REAL LIFE IS WEIRD!

Did you know that frogs are cannibals, fashion can be fatal and the dinosaurs never died? Or that redheads were once burned at the stake as witches? How about walking fish and talking eggs?

Find out what all the fuss is about. Collect the set of It's True! books and tantalise your friends with startling stories and far-out facts.

Coming soon: titles on THE SUPERNATURAL, SPACE, SPIES, POISONS, ANTARCTICA, BONES, JOKES, BUSHRANGERS

Find out all about it on
www.itstrue.com.au

John and Joshua Wright

PICTURES BY Joshua Wright

THE ROMANS WERE THE REAL GANGSTERS

ALLEN&UNWIN

Allen & Unwin
83 Alexander Street
Crows Nest NSW 2065
Australia
Phone: (61 2) 8425 0100
Fax: (61 2) 9906 2218
Email: info@allenandunwin.com
Web: www.allenandunwin.com

National Library of Australia
Cataloguing-in-Publication entry:

Wright, John, 1970– .
It's true! The Romans were the real gangsters.
Bibliography.
Includes index.
ISBN 1 74114 300 4.
1. Rome – History – Republic, 265–30 BC – Biography – Juvenile
literature. 2. Rome – History – Republic, 265–30 BC – Juvenile literature.
I. Wright, Joshua, 1973– . II. Title.
937.05

Series, cover and text design by Ruth Grüner
Cover illustration: Joshua Wright
Set in 12.5pt Minion by Ruth Grüner
Printed by McPherson's Printing Group

3 5 7 9 10 8 6 4 2

**Teaching notes for the It's True! series are available
on the website: www.itstrue.com.au**

CONTENTS

WHY ROMANS?

Why did we write about Romans? Because there are lots of great stories to tell about them!

Rome was the richest and most powerful city in the ancient world. The people who ran the place were gangsters: if you got in their way, you could expect a knife in the back (or front). Being a successful Roman meant being a tough guy. It meant putting yourself first, and everyone else last. For many years this gangster attitude served Rome well. But in 113 BC the Romans were in trouble. They'd forgotten how to be tough guys. The Roman army and its generals had gone soft, and were more interested in living the high life than in getting busy on the battlefield. Their timing couldn't have been worse! Tribes of hideous German barbarians were on the march . . .

I

IT'S TRUE:
GAIUS MARIUS
PICKED HIS NOSE

In the year 107 BC, Rome was in desperate trouble.
While its army was busy fighting King Jugurtha in
far-off North Africa, tribes of vicious barbarians were
gathering to the north of Italy, preparing to invade.
Over 200 000 in number, the barbarian warriors were
tough, hairy and motivated. They hated all things
civilised, and loved nothing better than fighting, killing
and knocking things over.

Rome was in panic. Terrified citizens ran
screaming through the streets. The city was defenceless,
and no one knew what to do about it. Everyone blamed

the government. People complained that the Roman Senate was full of tired old men who should have retired years ago. It was true. The frail and wrinkled Senators could only shrug their shoulders at the crisis: most of them hadn't picked up a sword in years.

When they'd finished blaming the government, people turned on the army. They whined and moaned that their generals had forgotten how to be tough and ruthless; and that Roman soldiers were more interested in living the high life in the city's extravagant baths and palaces than in slaughtering enemies on the battlefield. It was true: the barbarian hordes had already butchered one Roman army in Macedonia, and they had just finished wiping out another one.

Rome needed a hero.

It needed a new kind of leader: a man with fighting spirit. Someone who could whip the army into shape, take out King Jugurtha in Africa and sail home again to massacre the barbarians in North Italy. But where would Rome find such a man?

Gaius Marius was that man. Raised on a farm deep in the country, Marius was a rough and vulgar lad: the kind of boy who was cruel to animals and told dirty jokes while picking his nose. At school, Marius was always in trouble. He thought that education was a waste of time and his teachers were fools.

With such a rough and rugged attitude, it was no surprise to anyone that Marius left school with no education, no special skills and no career prospects. Still, his parents told him that he had to get a job. Marius could only hope that his bad attitude, his love of violence and cruelty, and his endless store of dirty jokes would make him a success in the Roman army.

They did. From the first day he joined the army, the other soldiers knew that Marius was different. He didn't seem to feel pain, and he had no pity for the weak.

In battle, Marius shrugged off wounds

as if they were paper cuts; and if his enemies begged
for mercy, he ran them through with his spear. A brutal
and efficient soldier, Marius was soon promoted to
General. When the Senate eventually placed him in
command of the war in North Africa, Marius chased
Jugurtha all over the desert, butchering the King's army,
burning African villages and telling rude jokes to his
own soldiers as he went along. Marius' campaign in
North Africa was so ferocious that King Jugurtha fled
the country and sought the protection of King Bocchus,
his father-in-law, across the African border.

With Jugurtha now in full retreat,
the people of Rome
knew that Marius
was the rugged,
feet-on-the-ground
kind of guy
they needed.
The trouble
was that Rome's old

and worn-out Senators didn't like Marius. As far as they were concerned, Marius was a badly behaved lout who belonged back on the farm with the rest of the pigs. But, with the barbarians marching on a defenceless Rome, the Senate had no choice. It passed a law making Marius the supreme commander of all Roman forces. Secretly though, they planned to sack Marius as soon as the crisis was over. 'Send him back to the barnyard,' they snickered.

While the Senate was plotting his downfall, Marius' army had surrounded King Bocchus' palace. Marius wasn't going to let Jugurtha escape. He laid siege to the palace, demanding that Bocchus hand his son-in-law over for punishment, or face the consequences.

While Marius waited for Bocchus' reply, he sat on his horse outside the palace telling dirty stories to his chief lieutenant, Lucius Sulla, who was supervising the siege. Sulla, like a good number-two guy, laughed

HA HA HA
HA HA
HA HA
HA

at Marius' jokes. But deep down, Sulla was secretly disgusted. 'Ignorant ape!', he mumbled. Sulla hated being second in charge.

Inside the palace, King Bocchus was frightened. He didn't want any trouble with Rome or Marius. But, family was family, and he agreed to let Jugurtha hide for a week or so. As the nights drew on, King Bocchus paced the halls of his palace wondering what to do next. Finally, he decided Jugurtha had to go. He sent a message to Sulla promising that he'd surrender his son-in-law to the Romans if Marius would leave his palace in peace.

Sulla knew he and Marius were already late for their date with the barbarians back in Italy. He accepted. And when Sulla returned from Bocchus' palace with Jugurtha in chains, the war in Africa was over, and the Roman army could go home.

Jugurtha was taken back to Rome and strangled to death. Marius oversaw the execution personally. And with one menace taken care of, it was time to move on to his next target – the barbarians.

CHOKE!
GASP!

But Marius knew that he had to make a few changes before his troops would be ready to face the vile barbarians. First, he improved their javelins. Marius replaced the iron rivets that held the spearhead to the javelin shaft with wooden rivets. By decreasing the javelin's strength at this point, he made sure the spearhead would break off on impact, making it impossible for the barbarians to throw the weapon back at the Romans. Next, Marius gave his men sharper swords and big new shields, which he bought at the city's expense. He also made each soldier carry his own equipment in a backpack, which removed the need for mules, carts and long baggage trains that only slowed the army down. Finally, Marius gave his legions the famous golden eagle symbol, which standard-bearers would carry into battle to inspire the soldiers. With better equipment, added mobility and a new image, the army was ready.

The barbarians were big, tough and hairy, but they were also quite stupid. As soon as they began their march on Rome, they divided themselves into two separate armies, reducing their strength by exactly one half. Marius knew that he had a much better chance of winning two quick battles against two smaller armies than one ferocious battle against a huge army. He seized his chance. Marius positioned his soldiers well, blocking the barbarians' path at the town of Aquae Sextiae. The barbarians charged as soon as they spotted Marius' soldiers. But their attack was hasty and unorganised. The barbarians hit the Roman line in dribs and drabs rather than as a single unified force. Inspired by their new eagle standards, Marius' soldiers held fast. The Romans massacred the barbarians by the thousands.

With their new backpacks and no baggage wagons to slow them down, Marius' army moved quickly around the countryside. They caught up with the second barbarian force further to the north, on the plains of Vercellae. This army was much bigger than the first one, but its barbarian warriors were just as stupid. The barbarian leaders threaded long chains through the belt buckles of their warriors to prevent anyone running away in the heat of battle. It was a crazy idea. Marius' soldiers simply knocked the barbarians down like dominoes. As they lay weighed down on the ground, struggling to stand up again, the Romans butchered the lot of them. Rome was saved.

Watching the victory from his horse, Marius told Sulla another dirty joke in celebration.

When Marius returned to Rome, he expected to get a hero's welcome. Instead, he got the sack! Sulla was tired of being the number-two guy. He could no longer bear Marius' disgusting stories,

nose-picking and all-round grossness. During the war Sulla had been secretly writing letters to people back in Rome spreading talk that he was the brains behind Marius' whole operation! Sulla claimed that it was he who had actually defeated Jugurtha and the barbarians, not Marius. Sulla even had a marble statue carved showing him capturing King Jugurtha in Africa! The frail old Senators lapped up Sulla's pathetic story. They had always hated Marius too. The Senate happily passed a new law placing Sulla in command of the army. As Marius sat in the Senate building complaining about the situation, the Senators laughed at him. 'Go back to pigs, nose-picker,' they heckled.

'Tell us a joke now, you loser!' As Marius strode out of the Senate House, he looked Sulla directly in the eyes.

'I'll be back,' he growled.

II

IT'S TRUE:

SULLA HATED BEING

NUMBER TWO

Lucius Sulla wanted to be the boss of everything.
He wanted to run the army. He wanted to run the
Senate. He wanted to run the whole city of Rome!
And Sulla was prepared to lie, cheat, bribe, steal,
and even murder his way to the top.

Sulla was also an extremely lucky guy. Things always
worked out for him. His first lucky break came when
he was a teenager. In Rome, money was important.
Nothing was free, and everything
could be bought.

If you wanted to be a judge, you had to pay your own salary. If you wanted to be a Senator, you had to buy your own votes. And if you wanted to be a general, you had to pay your army's wages. But Sulla's parents were extremely poor. Without money, Sulla's life was going nowhere. Yet, just when he seemed destined for failure, Sulla received news that he had inherited the wealthy estates of two distant aunties. Suddenly Sulla was rich. He was free to do whatever he wanted!

Sulla wanted to be the number-one guy in Rome. But first of all, he needed to be a general. So he joined the army and learned the ropes, serving as Marius' lieutenant in North Africa and Italy. But, with King Jugurtha dead and the barbarians lying massacred across two battlefields, Sulla thought it was time for Marius to step aside. After all, it was his turn to be General now. But Marius wouldn't have it. He loved being General.

Obviously there was only one thing to do. Sulla went behind Marius' back, and bribed the Senate to give him command of the army. It worked.

The Senate had always hated Marius anyway.

Rome's next target was King Mithradates of Pontus. To cut a long story short: Pontus was a small city on the other side of Greece. Mithradates, the King of Pontus, was a loud-mouthed yahoo who was getting on everybody's nerves. The Senate wanted him dead, and they wanted Sulla to do the hit. The only trouble was that Pontus was a long way from Rome. To put the hit on Mithradates, Sulla and his army needed to cross Greece. And to cross Greece, Sulla's troops would need food, water and shelter. Sulla asked the cities of Greece to help him but Athens, the largest and most important Greek city, told him to forget it.

GRRR!

COME UP HERE AND GET ME, CLOWN!

Sulla got angry. 'Wine-swilling, concrete-laying mongrels!' he mumbled. The Greeks didn't know it yet, but when Sulla got angry, a lot of people usually got killed. Sulla's army quickly surrounded Athens, bringing mighty catapults, huge rams and massive assault towers to bring down its concrete walls. But King Ariston, the leader of the Athenian Greeks, wasn't afraid. The walls of Athens were strong and high. He appeared daily on their highest tower, encouraging the Greeks to fight back, and shouting insults at Sulla. Ariston even made rude gestures at Sulla, and sang dirty songs about his wife. Sulla hated Ariston's songs. They reminded him of Marius' jokes.

In the beginning, the siege didn't go well for Sulla. The Greeks were extremely clever. After all, they had invented mathematics, philosophy, music and poetry. They were convinced that the Romans were far too stupid to pose a serious threat to Athens. The Greeks fired volleys of flaming arrows at Sulla's siege engines, burning his catapults, rams and assault towers into little black cinders. The Greeks knew that without them the siege was lost. But Sulla caught a lucky break. Some of his men overheard the Greek soldiers yelling at each other, arguing that Ariston had not properly fortified the wall at certain points. Screaming at each other at the tops of their voices, the noisy Greeks complained that if Sulla attacked one of these points, Athens would surely fall. The Greeks were extremely clever, but they also argued among themselves far too much.

Sulla took action. He gathered his men, attacked the wall at its weakest point, and knocked through a tremendous hole.

At midnight, Sulla stepped through the gap with his sword drawn. He was very, very angry with the Greeks for refusing to help him. He hadn't forgotten about Ariston's insults either! Sulla told his men to loot the gold from the Athenian temples and to whack every Greek in sight. It was a massacre. By sunrise, the slaughter could be measured by the flow of blood, which covered Athens' marketplace, and flowed out through the main gate and into the suburbs.

With the mayhem Sulla was causing in Greece, some of the Senators back in Rome began to dislike him. After all, what was supposed to be a simple hit on King Mithradates had turned into a Grecian bloodbath. Julius Caesar, who was a young Senator at the time, spoke out against Sulla in the Senate. Caesar said that Sulla had bribed his way to the top anyway, and should be thrown out of the army. The other Senators agreed.

Some of them thought they should put Marius back
in charge.

Back on his farm, Marius was getting old. He was
almost 60. He'd been unemployed for quite some time,
and had become bitter and twisted about things.
He got drunk nearly every day and he'd put on far
too much weight. When the Senate invited him back
to Rome, he accepted. But Marius wasn't about to say
'thank you'. Unemployment can drive a person crazy.
Marius came back to Rome with a sword in one hand,
a javelin in the other, and an angry mob of pig-farmers
behind him. He began by burning down Sulla's house.
Next, he ordered his mob to put the hit on all the
Senators who had given him the sack. Marius and the
pig-farmers whacked fourteen Senators, lopping off
their heads, and sticking them on the ends of their
spears. And when Marius entered the Senate
House to take control of the city, the angry

pig-farmers placed the fourteen severed heads on posts all around the chamber. It was a grisly sight. The remaining Senators were shocked. Marius had gone completely insane.

Back in Greece, Sulla's wife arrived at his headquarters complaining that Marius had burned down their house. Sulla got mighty angry. He forgot about getting to Pontus and loaded his troops back onto their ships. He would deal with that joke-telling nose-picker once and for all.

Sulla's army reached Roman shores to find that Marius had raised another army against him. The battle that followed was fierce. Sulla was almost killed by a stray javelin; but once again, his luck held. And when word came that his chief lieutenant, Marcus Crassus, had finally surrounded Marius' army, Sulla rushed forward,

...CALL IT THE ROMAN WAY OF GETTING AHEAD.

promising Marius' men he would let them go free if they surrendered. Foolishly, Marius' troops believed him. You see, Sulla was extremely angry with Marius' soldiers. And after they had given up all their weapons, Sulla ordered them massacred. 'Some people are just better off dead,' he told Crassus.

But Sulla was only beginning. As far as he was concerned, it was time to sort things out in Rome once and for all. He couldn't believe the Senators had sacked him and reappointed Marius because of one little massacre in Greece. Sulla decided that Rome's 'head-in-the-clouds' Senators simply had to go. He took out a scroll, wrote down the names of all the Senators he didn't like, and pinned it to a noticeboard in the city square. It was a hit list. A golden reward went to anyone who whacked a person listed on the scroll, no questions asked. It was a great way for local cut-throats to make fast money. Sulla wrote down another 200 names the following day, and then another 200 names the day after that.

After his hit lists were complete, and all the extremely annoying people on them had been brutally murdered, it was time to relax. Finally, Sulla was the ruler of Rome, and the boss of everything. He was no longer the number-two guy in the army. He had replaced all tired worn-out Senators with friends of his own. And with all the robberies, whackings and executions Sulla had ordered, the people of Rome were scared to death of him. Things ended well for Lucius Sulla. The good citizens of Rome hailed him as their leader, the keeper of the peace and an all-round great guy. And as the sun went down on another happy day in the glorious city of ancient Rome, everyone was in total and complete agreement that all the horrible, ruthless and nasty things that Sulla had done were really not so horrible after all.

III

IT'S TRUE:
MARCUS CRASSUS
LOST THE GOLDEN
EAGLES

Marcus Crassus was one of Sulla's best
friends. Sulla owed him big-time. When
Sulla's army returned from Greece to
fight Marius, Crassus helped Sulla's
soldiers surround and capture Marius'
army. So when the fighting was over,
Sulla let Crassus buy all the farms
and houses of people on his hit lists.

Crassus snapped them up at bargain prices. But Marcus Crassus was an extremely greedy fellow. He always wanted more. In fact, after Sulla had posted his third and final hit list in the city square, Crassus snuck up in the middle of the night, and secretly added a few extra names to it! Crassus thought that the more people who got whacked, the more houses and farms he could buy! Once all the people on Sulla's hit list had been taken out, Crassus was left as the richest man in ancient Rome. But never satisfied, greedy Crassus ran all sorts of dodgy scams to make him richer still. One of his biggest scams was the Roman Fire Brigade.

Most Roman houses were made of wood. They were built in large apartment blocks, very close together, and up to five storeys high. Fires were a constant risk. Yet, where the average Roman saw a potential disaster, Crassus saw a business opportunity. He already owned thousands of slaves.

Crassus thought that if he trained a few of them to be firemen, he could make some fast cash. Crassus bought his firemen shiny new hats, smart uniforms and long ladders. He even bought them a horse-drawn fire engine. The scam was that Crassus' fire brigade only put out fires in houses that belonged to Crassus. If anyone else's home caught fire, Crassus' men would arrive at the scene and offer to buy it. If the owner sold the house to Crassus, they would put out the fire. If the owner didn't sell, they would let the house burn to the ground. Of course Crassus offered miserable prices for burning houses, but most owners sold anyway. They had little choice. Crassus' fire brigade was the only one in town. In a few years, Crassus owned nearly all the houses in Rome. He made a fortune charging everyone rent.

Money, houses, farms and fire brigades weren't enough for Crassus. More than anything else, he wanted to be a great general – just like his old pal Sulla. One day, if he played his cards right, he might even rule Rome! And after Sulla had died of old age, Crassus got his chance.

The city of Rome was full of slaves. In the ancient world, owning a slave was like owning a car – you just had to have one! The average Roman citizen couldn't get any housework done without a slave or two around. The trouble is that nobody actually enjoys being a slave. In 73 BC, a very badly behaved slave named Spartacus busted out of gladiator school and started **a slave rebellion.** Spartacus raised an army of almost 70 000 slaves! He defeated two Roman armies sent to destroy him. Spartacus set up a hideout in the south of Italy. His men began to make swords and shields for the battles ahead. Their plan was to fight their way out of Italy and free themselves of Rome and slavery forever. But back in Rome, the Senators were angry. With all the slaves hiding out at Spartacus' fort, there was nobody left in Rome to do the housework!

The Senate put out a contract on Spartacus, and asked Crassus to do the hit.

ROMAN WIFE

HEY! WHERE DO YOU THINK YOU'RE GOING, MISTER? YOU STILL HAVEN'T FINISHED THE DISHES!

SLAVE №7

Crassus was eager to prove himself in battle.
He took command of the army and marched his
soldiers south. He made camp very close to Spartacus'
hideout, hoping to tempt the slaves into an unplanned
attack. It worked. Full of impudence, Spartacus and
the slaves charged Crassus' army with all their might.
Spartacus ran directly towards Crassus, wanting to
challenge him to the kind of fight that old gladiators
liked best: a man-to-man duel. He didn't get far.
Spartacus slew a couple of Roman soldiers, but all
the others soon chopped him into very small pieces.
Spartacus' slave army didn't last much longer. Most
of them were killed in the battle. And Crassus had the
leftovers crucified all along the roadside on his way
back to Rome.

With the renegade slaves nailed to wooden crosses
all up and down Rome's highways, Crassus was feeling
pretty good about himself. He wanted more. He came
up with the idea of invading Parthia. The Parthians
lived in Mesopotamia near the Euphrates River, in
what we know today as northern Iraq. Rome had
nothing against the Parthians, but Crassus thought it

might be a good idea to massacre them all the same. The Senate agreed. As Sulla had taught them: the odd massacre here and there was a great way of keeping the local populations in check. The Senate gave Crassus another army, and ordered him to whack the Parthians. But Julius Caesar, who was a close friend of Crassus, advised him to be extremely careful. Caesar was an expert general, and he knew that the Parthians didn't fight fair. 'Fighting a bunch of slaves is easy,'

Caesar warned Crassus. 'Fighting the Parthians will be something else.' Crassus didn't listen. 'Relax, Julius,' he replied, 'I'll whack those Parthians in a month.'

Arriving in the hot Iraqi desert, Crassus marched his army along the base of a mountain range, looking for the Parthians. Now, the Parthian army was quite small, numbering only about 12 000. Crassus' army was huge: he had over 50 000 soldiers. Convinced he'd win easily, Crassus took his scouts out into the desert to look for the Parthians, hoping to challenge them to a decisive battle. But they were nowhere to be seen. Crassus found only the hoofprints of Parthian horses. It was hot out in the desert too. Crassus was sweating like a pig. And back at camp, his army was running low on water. He had to find the Parthians soon.

While Crassus wondered what to do next, a local chieftain named Ariamnes drifted into the Roman camp, saying he knew where the Parthian army was hiding. Ariamnes offered to lead Crassus right to them. Hot and thirsty, Crassus accepted. Leaving the shelter of the mountains behind them, the Romans took up their golden eagle standards and followed Ariamnes

out into the desert. Now, Roman soldiers wore bulky
leather armour and metal helmets. They carried
heavy swords and large shields. And the Romans liked
to march around on foot. The Parthian army hated
marching. They rode horses. They wore light armour
and carried no swords, no shields; all they had were
bows and arrows. The Roman army packed a mighty
punch; but the Parthian army was extremely fast,
and could keep well out of sight of Crassus' army.
After a few days marching under the hot desert sun,
the Romans had found nothing but more hoofprints.

It was a trap. Ariamnes was really working
for the Parthians. After he had led the Roman army
far out into the desert, he disappeared. Moments
later, the Parthian army charged over the dunes, firing
their bows from horseback. The sky rained arrows,

and Crassus' men dropped like flowers in a hailstorm. When the Romans marched forward to attack, the Parthians rode off into the distance, firing as they went. And whenever the Romans paused to rest, the Parthians returned to shower them with even more arrows. In the end, it was a slaughter. Crassus' army never even got close to the Parthians.

Surena, the Parthian General, offered to make peace with Crassus. Hot, thirsty and confused, Crassus accepted and rode out to meet him. It was another Parthian trap. As Crassus climbed down from his saddle, Parthian soldiers grabbed him, jabbed a spear into his belly and chopped his head off.

When news of Crassus' death reached his men, they panicked. Soldiers dropped their swords, shields and even their golden eagle standards, and fled for the mountains, dodging Parthian arrows as they ran. Few of them ever saw Rome again.

Surena watched from his saddle as the disaster unfolded. With Crassus' severed head tucked neatly under his arm, Surena reached down and plucked the golden eagle standards from the sand.

Surena sent the standards and Crassus' head to Hyrodes, the King of Parthia. When they arrived at his palace, King Hyrodes was overjoyed. Dusting the sand from the standards, Hyrodes placed them on the wall directly behind his throne. Clapping his hands, the King ordered music played, and called for his dancing girls. He threw them the head. Jumping and spinning on their heels, the Parthian dancers caught the prize and gracefully worked what was left of Crassus into their routine.

IV

IT'S TRUE:
PUBLIUS CLODIUS
CAUSED A PUBLIC
SCANDAL

When news that Crassus had lost the golden eagle standards finally reached Rome, there was public outrage. All across the city, people cried out for revenge. Everyone wanted the eagle standards back. It was a civic disgrace. The whole of Rome agreed: 'Nobody whacks our guys!' But for the moment, revenge against the Parthians would have to wait – Rome was caught up in a domestic scandal. Julius Caesar's wife was about to run off with another man!

Publius Clodius was the best-looking guy in Rome. He was so handsome his friends gave him the nickname '*Pulcher*', which is Roman for beautiful. Clodius came from a wealthy Roman family. He had money, style, a big house and a fast chariot. Women just loved him. Clodius was so popular with the ladies that even Pompeia, Julius Caesar's gorgeous wife, had a crush on him. Most Romans would have been very worried if Caesar's wife took a shine to them, but Clodius didn't care. He was a stress-free guy. As far as he was concerned, he could do whatever he wanted.

While Caesar was away on business in France, Pompeia was stuck at home with nothing to do. Clodius already knew that she liked him. And with Caesar busy focusing on his career, Pompeia was a juicy apple ripe for the picking.

COME AND GET ME, LADIES

Now, in ancient Rome, the gods were very important. People worried about what would happen if they stopped worshipping the gods. Hoping to keep the gods happy, the Romans held religious festivals all the time: festivals for Mars the god of war, festivals for Venus the goddess of love, and festivals for Jupiter the father of all the gods. One night, Pompeia, Caesar's mother Aurelia and all their friends were celebrating the sacred festival of the goddess Bona at Caesar's house. Bona was the 'Good Goddess', the Roman goddess of fertility and healing. On the first of May every year, Roman women would gather at the house of a friend to bless snakes, play music and sing songs in Bona's honour. Roman women worried that if they didn't worship Bona they might not have healthy babies. Clodius knew men were not allowed at Bona's festival, so he guessed it would be the perfect time to catch up with Pompeia.

Disguising himself in women's clothes and make-up, Clodius snuck into Caesar's house. But, as he wandered about looking for Pompeia, he bumped into one of her maids. Clodius pulled the hood of his cloak down to hide his face. The maid asked him where he was going. When Clodius offered a reply, she immediately recognised his deep, manly voice. The maid dropped her basket and ran: 'There's **a man in the house!** There's a man in the house!' she cried. Pompeia, Aurelia and all their friends called a halt to the festival. With a man in the house, the ceremony was ruined. The women locked all the doors and searched everywhere. When they discovered Clodius hiding in Pompeia's bedroom, they beat him with sticks and brooms and drove him out into the night.

The next day, the scandal was all over the city. Clodius had offended the gods. It was serious business.

He was hauled off to prison to await trial. But remember, Clodius was a stress-free guy. He couldn't care less about the gods and their ceremonies. He didn't care what the law said about the gods either. Clodius knew that to get out of jail, all he had to do was invent a few believable lies, and things would be fine.

Clodius' trial was big news. When

the case eventually came to court, Clodius defended himself by claiming that he wasn't actually in Rome at the time of the festival. Clodius said that he was away in Greece, and that someone else must have broken into Pompeia's house. It was an excellent lie. A lot of people believed it. But things turned ugly for Clodius when his friend Marcus Cicero stepped into the witness box. You see, Clodius had a gorgeous younger sister named Clodia. Cicero was crazy about her! He kept visiting her, buying her presents and taking her out to parties. Until his wife Terentia found out! Terentia was a nasty piece of work. She took her revenge against Cicero and Clodia by forcing her husband to testify against Clodius in court. Spineless, slimy Cicero caved in to his wife's demands. 'Yes, dear . . . of course,

my sweet', the weak-willed creature told her. In court, Cicero testified that Clodius was lying. Cicero claimed that on the morning of 1 May Clodius had come to visit him at his home to discuss some business matters. The courtroom was in uproar! Clodius exploded from the dock: 'I'll get you, you dirty rat!' Slimy Cicero slunk out of the witness box. He had just ratted on one of his best friends.

In ancient Rome, jurors wrote their final decision – guilty or not guilty – by scratching the words into wax tablets. But when the jury members delivered their verdict at Clodius' trial, their writing was so hard to read that no one could actually understand what the tablets said. But what people didn't realise was that the jury had done it on purpose. Clodius had bribed every one of them!

Out of prison and back on the street, Clodius wanted payback. He was determined to get even with that so-called friend of his for ratting on him. Clodius invented some fake charges against Cicero and brought him to trial. But Cicero was too clever for that. He dressed himself in rags, and leaving his hair unbrushed and his beard unshaved, started walking around Rome begging for sympathy. The plan worked. Almost 20 000 people followed his example and dressed in rags, without brushing their hair, or shaving their beards. It was a symbol they were on his side.

CICERO GROUPIES

Clodius was furious. He dropped the court case and simply hired a gang of thugs to follow Cicero through the city and throw mud at him wherever he went. Just for good measure, Clodius told his thugs to beat Cicero up whenever he did his shopping. Pretty soon Cicero was being harassed and beaten up all over town. He had no choice but to leave Rome.

Clodius still wasn't satisfied. After Cicero had gone, Clodius burnt down Cicero's house and offered all his belongings for public sale. Next, he ordered his gang of thugs to beat up all of Cicero's supporters in the Senate. If that wasn't enough, Clodius set fire to the Senate house. Clodius laughed himself silly as high-and-mighty Senators fled the building with their clothes on fire. The Senate House was reduced to a pile of ashes.

Clodius' cycle of revenge was spiralling out of control. The Senators decided that he had to be taken out – permanently. 'Some people are just better off dead,' they all agreed. And anyway, Rome had Crassus' missing golden eagles to worry about now. The Senate put out a contract on Clodius, and asked Titus Milo to do the hit. Milo had his own gang of thugs, and it was much bigger than Clodius' gang. Pretty soon, Rome was consumed in bitter street battles between the two rival gangs. And when Clodius was cut to shreds in a street fight just outside the city, nobody in Rome cared much at all.

V

IT'S TRUE: JULIUS CAESAR WAS A TREND-SETTER

Julius Caesar also gave evidence at Clodius' trial.
He told the jury he knew nothing about Clodius
sneaking into his house, but that he had divorced his
wife Pompeia all the same: 'Some people are just better
off divorced,' he said. Caesar had returned from France
around this time because he wanted revenge against
the Parthians for killing his friend Crassus. Caesar was
one of the best generals in the whole of the ancient
world. He had just finished massacring the native
tribes in France and Spain, and he'd even put the hit on
some other Roman generals who wanted the Parthian

contract for themselves. Now, Caesar wanted to rule **the whole Roman Empire**, and planned to let nothing get in his way.

War and destruction were in Caesar's blood. After all, Caesar was Marius' nephew. And just like his uncle Marius, Caesar was as tough as nails. He loved whacking people and telling dirty jokes. But Caesar was also very different from Marius. He had paid attention to his teachers at school. He got along splendidly with almost everyone. And Caesar never picked his nose.

Caesar was stylish too – a real trend-setter. He was a tall, handsome man who kept his hair neatly trimmed and his face smoothly shaved. Caesar was so keen on his appearance he even had his personal hairdressers pluck out the hairs from his arms and legs with tweezers!

THAT PRETTY
BOY IS
CRUISING
FOR A
BRUISING!

Caesar liked wearing the latest fashions too. Your average Roman citizen got around town in a loose white robe called a toga, but Caesar wanted to stand out. He had purple stripes sewn around the edges of his toga, and purple fringes about his wrists. He also wore a belt around the outside of his toga. People thought he looked a little weird, but Caesar didn't mind. He thought that everybody would be wearing belts with purple-fringed togas one day.

Sulla had never liked Caesar's glamour-boy looks. When Sulla made himself ruler of Rome and was busy whacking everybody he didn't like, Caesar was still a teenager. Sulla thought long and hard about whether to put young Caesar on his hit list. Caesar was flashy, which really annoyed Sulla. Caesar was also Marius' nephew, which annoyed Sulla even more. And Caesar had spoken out against him in the Senate, which was pretty much the limit. But in the end, Sulla couldn't make up his mind. Caesar was probably just an upstart teenager. And anyway, whacking someone just because they dressed funny and came from a bad family seemed a bit much – even for Sulla. But when young Caesar heard that Sulla didn't like him, he was very worried. He knew that when Sulla got angry, a lot of people usually got killed. Caesar didn't want to be one of them. He collected his hairdressers, hired a boat and sailed away to Greece.

Caesar may have run from Sulla, but he was no coward. Like his uncle Marius before him, Caesar was one tough dude. When Sulla had finished killing everybody he didn't like, Caesar returned to Rome.

Sailing back through the Greek islands, Caesar's ship was attacked by pirates.

MAYBE WE'D GO FASTER IF WE BUILT MORE THAN ONE SAIL ONTO THESE THINGS?

THAT'S JUST CRAZY TALK.

The pirates took young Caesar prisoner, hoping to extract a ransom from his family. The pirates demanded a small fortune in gold for his safe return. Caesar just laughed at them. He called them fools and barbarians. They didn't understand his true value. Caesar said he was actually worth a very large fortune in gold!

While his family was busy raising the money, Caesar was allowed to roam freely around the ship, joining in the pirates' games, and telling all the dirty jokes that his uncle Marius had told him as a boy. The pirates soon liked him so much, they asked him to join their gang. But young Caesar refused – he hated pirates. And he warned them that after he was free, he would hunt them down and have them all nailed to wooden crosses. The pirates fell down laughing at Caesar and his sad little threats. After all, they thought, he was just an upstart teenager with a big mouth.

He didn't know anything.

How wrong they were.

With the ransom paid, the pirates set young Caesar free. Caesar immediately hired a fleet

AWWW, LOOK. HE REALLY DOES CARE!

of ships and a crew of mercenaries. Caesar and his mercenaries scoured the Mediterranean Sea looking for the pirates. He had a promise to keep. And he wanted his money back too. In only a few weeks, Caesar caught up with the pirates, sank their ship and took them all prisoner. He had promised to crucify the pirates, and crucify them he did. But showing mercy, young Caesar ordered his men to cut the pirates' throats beforehand in order to spare them the awful pain of being nailed to wooden crosses. After all, Caesar was a 'people guy'.

As the years went by and Caesar got older, he started to go bald. Caesar really, really loved his hair. And as it began to fall out, he got himself into an awful panic.

Caesar's hairdressers found a temporary solution. They brushed his remaining hair forward over his scalp. But it didn't work. Rome was a windy city, and the comb-over quickly became a messy blow-over. Marc Antony, Caesar's number-two guy, had a brilliant idea! Antony encouraged Caesar to wear a crown of laurel leaves around his head in order to keep his comb-over safe from the wind. Antony's idea worked. Caesar was stoked. 'Antony,' he said, 'you're a flaming genius!'

But the laurel crown created major problems. In ancient Rome, kings were not cool. The Romans hated the idea of being ruled by a king. Kings were always in your face, ordering you around, telling you what to do and making you bow down in front of them. The Romans didn't like bowing down to anybody. And the trouble was that Caesar's laurel wreath looked exactly like a king's crown. The high-and-mighty Senators all agreed Caesar must be trying to set himself up as the King of Rome.

There were other problems too. In his mad, revenge-driven frenzy against Cicero, Clodius had burnt the Senate House. As a result, the Senators were forced to hold their meetings in a nearby theatre. Nobody liked the theatre. It had cold, hard marble seats. Caesar complained that the seats made his bottom go numb. Marc Antony solved the problem by having a special chair made, just for Caesar. Marc Antony always tried hard to impress his boss. The new chair was made from imported wood, inlaid with gold, and had soft purple cushions. It was very comfy. Caesar was stoked. 'Antony,' he said, 'you're a flaming genius!'

COME NOW, FELLOWS.
YOU'RE IMAGINING
THINGS. WE'RE ALL
JUST ONE BIG TEAM
AROUND HERE...
RIGHT?

But what Antony didn't realise was that the new chair looked just like a king's throne. What's more, Caesar liked to sit in his chair at the front of the theatre, because, as he explained, he could not very well move aside the heavy marble seats in the audience to make room. So when Caesar sat on his wonderful new chair at the front of the theatre wearing his laurel crown and his fancy toga, he really did look like a king holding court. It was too much for the other Senators to bear.

Calling themselves 'the conspirators', a group of disgruntled Senators decided Caesar's time was up. They all agreed to do the hit together. One morning, just as Caesar took his seat at the front of the theatre, the renegade group gathered round him. Suddenly Caesar realised his mistake: he should never have listened to Antony. But it was too late now. One of the conspirators grabbed Caesar by his toga. Another stabbed him in the neck.

HMMM... MAYBE THEY JUST DIDN'T CARE FOR PURPLE?..

MARC ANTONY

52

The conspirators thrust 23 daggers into Caesar's body. His clothes were ruined. Image-conscious to the end, as Caesar fell to the ground, he wrapped the top half of his toga over his head, hiding his baldness from the mob. After he collapsed, the conspirators fled the scene, leaving Marc Antony to pick up the pieces. As his life-blood poured out onto the floor, the dying Caesar rested his head in Antony's arms.

'Antony,' Caesar said, 'you're a flaming idiot!'

VI

IT'S TRUE: MARC ANTONY WAS A FLAMING IDIOT

Marius, Sulla, Crassus and Caesar were all dead.
Rome was running out of generals. And with the
Parthians still holding Crassus' golden eagle standards,
the civic disgrace remained. Rome couldn't rest.
Marc Antony put himself forward as the next shining
star of the Roman military. But no one took Antony
seriously. He was an idiot. Everyone knew it.

Marc Antony loved three things: music, booze
and parties. When things got funky, no one partied
harder than Antony. He loved to sizzle. In fact, Marc
Antony established the world's very first nightclub

in the heart of ancient Rome. He bought an old house on the prestigious Palatine Hill, and converted it into Rome's first music and dance club. 'Antony on Top' pumped night after night.

Antony always stayed out late. He arrived for work drunk practically every day. On one occasion, Antony was due to give an important speech in the city square, but the previous night he had been boozing it up at a local comedian's wedding. Next morning, as he stepped up to the podium to deliver the speech, his friends tried to restrain him. Antony pushed them away with a drunken growl. Looking out over the crowd, he swayed for a moment, and without even managing to utter a single word, he vomited all over the people in the front row. It was disgusting.

Even when Antony wasn't drunk on the job, he still acted as though he was. After Caesar's death, the man was an emotional wreck. In fact, when he spoke at Caesar's funeral, he was so upset that he incited a riot. Antony had been one of the few people who adored Caesar's stylish ways. Before speaking a word to the mourners, Antony grabbed the purple-fringed toga from Caesar's body, and held it up for the crowd to see. Showing them blood-stained holes left by the many daggers, and calling the conspirators villains and

murderers, Antony whipped up the crowd into a mad frenzy. They gathered flaming torches from Caesar's funeral pyre and set off to burn the conspirators in their houses.

The riot became a general uprising against Caesar's murderers, and it pushed Antony to the forefront of Roman politics. He soon became friendly with Caesar's adopted heir, Augustus Caesar. With all the conspirators burned to death, Antony and Augustus emerged as the two most powerful people in Rome. Now, by 42 BC, Rome's Empire stretched all the way from Spain in the west to Syria in the east. It was far too big an operation for one person to manage. Antony and Augustus divided the world between them.

While Augustus would stay in Italy to manage Rome and the west, Antony would head east to deal with the Parthians and snatch back Crassus' golden eagle standards. It was a brilliant plan. Only a complete and utter idiot could possibly ruin it.

Antony promised Augustus that he would put the hit on the Parthians as soon as possible. But that was before he met Cleopatra. Queen Cleopatra of Egypt was okay-looking, but that wasn't her real appeal. She was as sharp as a tack, witty, charming and mind-blowingly interesting. Men just loved her. When Antony first headed east, he sent Cleopatra big-headed letters, demanding she come to meet him in Greece. Cleopatra ignored them. Instead, she tricked Antony into running to see *her*.

First, Cleopatra sailed across the Mediterranean to Greece in her golden pleasure barge. As she drew near the shore, braziers of perfume on the deck burned smoky, exotic scents across the beach, and crowds gathered to watch her sail by. Antony was among them. Cleopatra's golden barge flew purple sails, and was driven by oars of silver that dipped the water in time with music played on harps. When Antony first caught a glimpse of Cleopatra, she was lying outstretched on the deck under a canopy of golden cloth being fanned by handsome slaves while her maids, dressed as sea nymphs, held the rudder. It was such an amazing spectacle that idiot Antony totally lost control of himself.

Unlike Antony, Augustus was a thorough professional. He had organised a huge Roman army for Antony to lead, and he had already sent it to the Parthian border. The army included 8000 Armenian horsemen, led by Artavasdes the King of Armenia, who would be able to pursue the mounted Parthian archers and force them to fight. Victory would be a snap. All Antony had to do was turn up. But now that he'd met Cleopatra, lovesick Antony forgot all about the war. He boarded the Queen's golden barge and sailed away to Egypt.

By the time the army was in place on the Parthian border, Antony was on holiday in Egypt. When he eventually dragged himself away from Cleopatra and arrived at the border to take command, all he could

do was daydream about his beautiful Egyptian queen. Artavasdes soon realised that Antony was useless. The Armenian king packed up camp and took his cavalry home. The campaign was ruined.

Back in Rome, Augustus was furious. Antony had not only ruined the war; he was actually supposed to be engaged to Augustus' sister Octavia. Antony's affair with Cleopatra was a grave insult to Augustus' family. Augustus had had enough. 'Don't worry, he'll never get away with this!' he told his crying sister. Augustus convinced the Senate to put a contract out on Antony, and even offered to kill the love-sick fool himself. Augustus told the Senate that Cleopatra was just as much to blame. She had obviously bewitched the hapless idiot with spells and potions.

When Antony wasn't drunk or love-sick, he could be quite a reasonable general, but by this time, he had completely lost touch with reality. He was obsessed with ships and golden barges. He came up with the crazy idea of building huge, powerful warships with which he and Cleopatra could take over the whole world. Augustus had the much more reasonable idea of building many small, faster ships to sink Antony's wooden monsters. The two navies eventually met in battle at Actium. For a time, it looked as though Antony and Cleopatra might actually win the day. However, during the fighting, Antony caught sight of Cleopatra's ship hoisting its sail and heading for the horizon. Making a critical blunder, idiot Antony abandoned the battle and followed Cleopatra. With no one left in command, his navy was quickly defeated.

When Augustus had sunk the last of Antony's ships, he sailed to Egypt in search of the runaway couple. Augustus arrived in Alexandria to find Antony already dead. Apparently, when Antony arrived in Egypt he'd heard a rumour Cleopatra had died at sea. Mad with grief, he killed himself with his own sword without bothering to find out whether the rumours were true. 'What an idiot,' said Augustus as looked over Antony's bloodied corpse.

Sure enough, Augustus found Cleopatra very much alive. She even tried to make friends, telling him that she'd only just realised that Antony was a complete loser. Cleopatra said that they should simply leave the past in the past, and get on with their lives. It sounded like a good idea. The trouble was that 'live-and-let-live' was not exactly the Roman way of doing things.

And when Cleopatra discovered that Augustus' only interest in her was to drive her chained and naked through the streets of Rome for the amusement of its citizens, she decided that there was nothing for it but to kill herself too.

VII
IT'S TRUE:
CALIGULA WENT
COMPLETELY MAD

After Augustus Caesar defeated Antony and Cleopatra, he set himself up as the ruler of Rome. But Augustus didn't call himself Emperor. He was much too smart for that! Augustus knew that kings and emperors were not cool. He had learned from his uncle Julius' mistakes. Instead, he called himself *Princeps*, which is Roman-speak for 'first man'. Augustus knew that being a good *Princeps* meant not dressing in fancy clothes and sitting on flash chairs, but living modestly and staying out of sight. Most of all, being a good *Princeps* meant pulling all the strings in Rome, but appearing not to. And to the untrained eye, it really did look as though the Senate was still running things in Rome; but behind the scenes, **Augustus was controlling everything.** He was the puppet-master. Nobody did anything without his say-so.

Augustus was exceptionally good at being Emperor. Everyone was afraid of him – even the Parthians. As soon as he took over, they gave Crassus' golden eagle standards straight back, no questions asked. They just prayed that he wouldn't decide to whack them for having been so slow about it.

When Augustus died, his adopted son Tiberius took over. Like his father, Tiberius was an expert puppet-master. The Roman Empire prospered. Tiberius saved up piles of cash, and made Rome the richest city in the world. But, when Tiberius died, and his grandson Gaius Caligula took over, things went downhill fast.

Caligula was insane – truly and utterly insane.

He had long conversations with his pet horse. He declared himself a god. He built temples to himself, and sacrificed small furry animals. Caligula built his horse a magnificent house, and held dinner parties inside. He even thought about making his beloved steed a Senator. The man was such a lunatic that he wanted to cut his wife Caesonia into little pieces so that he could discover why he loved her so much.

Gaius Caligula was not born mad. He came from a good family and went to military school. His father, Germanicus Caesar, was a famous Roman general who raised his son in military camps. When Gaius was just a boy, Germanicus bought him a small suit of armour, complete with boots and a helmet. As Gaius strolled around the camp dressed in his armour, Germanicus'

soldiers would laugh. They gave Gaius the nickname 'Caligula', which is Roman (or Latin) for 'Little Boots'.

After his father died, Caligula went to live with his grandfather Tiberius. By this time, Tiberius was an old man. He had to nominate a new Emperor to pull the strings in Rome after he died. He was thinking about recommending Caligula, but he worried there was something seriously wrong with his grandson. Caligula was disturbed by strange dreams in which he had long talks with the ocean. He never slept for more than three hours, and he was terribly afraid of thunder and lightning. At the first sign of a storm, he would wrap his head in a cloak and run inside screaming. Tiberius feared that he might be raising a psycho.

He was! By the time Tiberius was on his deathbed, Caligula even looked insane: his eyes spun like whirlpools and his tongue drooped out of the corner of his mouth. Hoping to ease his madness, Caligula's wife Caesonia provided him with special potions, but these only threw her husband into fits of rage, which permanently warped his face and features. As the insanity slowly claimed him, Caligula, with mad eyes flashing and twisted mouth dribbling, would stand in front of the mirror for hours, laughing and cackling. He was delighted with his hideous appearance. He thought he looked handsome!

The Roman people guessed something was not quite right with Caligula. After taking over from Tiberius, Caligula appeared in public dressed in bizarre cloaks, brightly embroidered with jewels. Sometimes Caligula wore a girl's dress, or pretended to be a god by gluing a golden beard to his chin and carrying a wooden thunderbolt. Other times he wore a bikini and told everyone that his name was really not Caligula but Venus (Venus was the goddess of love).

Late one night, Caligula summoned all the Senators to his palace. Thinking the city was under attack or something, the Senators hurried to the palace and sat in Caligula's audience chamber. They waited. And they waited. Then they waited some more. Suddenly Caligula burst out from behind a curtain. Dressed in a golden shirt and jewel-encrusted cloak, he skipped around the chamber playing a flute. Taking a quick bow, he cast the wooden instrument aside, and produced some castanets. Springing into the air, Caligula click-clacked his way through a breathtaking Spanish dance. After a dramatic high-kicking finish, Caligula took a final bow and went back to bed without saying a word. The Senators were speechless. There could no longer be any doubt: the Emperor was bonkers!

At this stage, Caligula was only singing and dancing, so his insanity wasn't really hurting anyone. But after he decided he wanted to be a god, and discovered an interest in torture and executions, things started to get out of hand.

The gods were very important in ancient Rome. The Romans liked to make statues of their favourite gods. All over Rome there were statues of Jove, Venus, Mars and Mercury. But, after Caligula declared himself a god too, he replaced the heads of all Rome's statutes with marble images of his own head. Next, he built a temple to himself in the city square, and placed a life-size statue of himself inside. While priests sacrificed flamingoes, peacocks, turkeys and pheasants to him on the temple's marble altar, Caligula would dance around the statue playing his flute. One day, when Caligula was making the sacrifice himself, he took up the sacrificial axe, brought it down on one of his priests, and chopped him into pieces. Caligula tried to laugh it off as all just a big joke, but the onlookers were horrified!

Things got worse. At the opening of a bridge

outside the city, Caligula cut the ribbon, and then ordered his guards to hurl his invited guests into the river. Back in Rome, when he discovered that a slave had stolen silverware from one of his horse's dinner parties, Caligula ordered the slave's hands cut off, and had them dangled on a chain around the slave's neck for all the guests to see. At the gym, when a gladiator was teaching him how to use a sword, Caligula ran his instructor through with a spear. It was becoming clear to everyone that Caligula's madness required 'treatment'.

Although the ancient Romans believed in treating the mentally ill, they didn't believe in providing patients with counselling and therapy. Typically, they believed in forming a conspiracy against the patient, and planting ten or twenty knives into the patient's chest.

One morning, after another sleepless night, Caligula was strolling through his palace. As he stopped to speak with some actors in the garden, two of his guards crept up behind him. The first struck him around the neck with a sword; the second stabbed him in the chest with a dagger. Mortally wounded, Caligula fell to the ground and cried out for his wife. The guards eyed each other. The Emperor was still alive. He needed further treatment. Working together, they hacked away at him, delivering another 30 wounds. When the Emperor's body finally went limp, the guards smiled at each other. Crazy Caligula was finally cured.

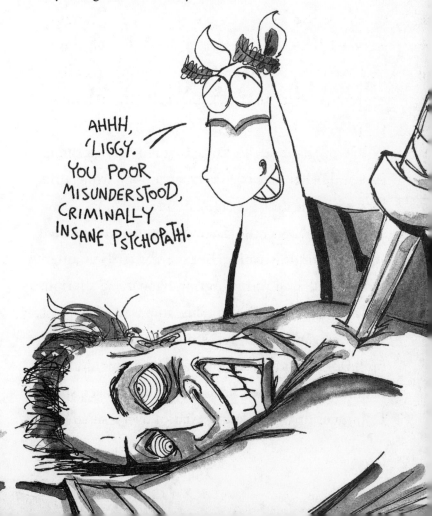

VIII

IT'S TRUE:
NERO'S MOTHER WAS
REALLY ASKING FOR IT!

With Caligula dead, his uncle Claudius Caesar thought that he'd better take over as *Princeps* for a while. And for a while, he did.

Caligula had a little sister, Agrippina, who seemed very sweet and charming. But she was really an utter terror. While still young, Agrippina married a serious boozehound named Domiticus, who was known to kill his servants if they refused to share a drink with him. Domiticus and Agrippina often drank themselves stupid together. Once, just for a bit of drunken sport, Domiticus drove the family chariot over a small boy playing beside the road, crushing him to death. When they weren't drinking, arguing or beating each other up, Domiticus and Agrippina found time to have a child. They called him Nero. Fortunately for Nero, his father Domiticus had drunk himself to death by the time he turned three. But that left his mother in charge, and she was as crazy as her brother.

Little Nero had always dreamed of being a singing star. As a boy, he sang and recited poetry at public theatres. But his mother wanted him to be the next Emperor of Rome, not some hopeless musician. As Caligula's little sister, Nero's mum had important connections. Claudius Caesar was her uncle. After Domiticus died, Agrippina persuaded her uncle Claudius to marry her and adopt Nero as his son and heir. Claudius was getting old. He needed a bit of loving, so he agreed. But Agrippina was only using Claudius to help make Nero the next Emperor. When Nero turned seventeen, Agrippina fed Claudius some poisoned mushrooms. He died within seconds. At seventeen years of age, Nero became the new Emperor of Rome. But he wasn't very interested in his job.

All Nero wanted to do was sing.

Nero completely ignored his new responsibilities as Emperor and focused on his music career instead. He hired Terpnus, a famous musical coach, to teach him to sing and play the harp. Day after day, Nero and Terpnus sat practising. Nero became so serious about his singing that he refused to eat fruit, thinking that the juice would damage his vocal cords. He even refused to speak without Terpnus' approval.

But while Nero was working on his music, his mother was always embarrassing him and badgering him about being a committed Emperor. She kept on that he was a drunken fool just like his father. But what hurt most of all was that she said he couldn't sing for nuts.

As months passed, Nero's singing improved. When his student was finally ready, Terpnus approved Nero's plan for a concert tour of Greece. Nero performed in the Greek cities of Athens, Olympia and Corinth. People flocked to the auditoriums. And when they were full, Nero's bouncers locked the doors. While he was on stage, no one was allowed to leave the theatre: no ducking out to the toilet, no going for snacks, no nothing. Nero would perform for up to ten hours, too! And if the audience tried to leave, Nero's bouncers told them to go back to their seats and enjoy the show – or else.

Nero didn't stop at concert tours. He invented his own musical talent quest called *Neronia*.

Neronia was an open-air music competition, in which the best musicians from around the ancient world would compete for a laurel crown. Nero always entered, and he always sang first. During the backstage warm-ups, he would closely watch the other contestants. If they were better than him, he would abuse and threaten them, or even bribe them to clear out of town.

Nero put pressure on the judges too. He hired thousands of people to cheer him whenever he performed. He taught them different kinds of applause: from simple clapping and cheering to more aggressive whooping and hollering, all the way up to totally wild yelling and screaming. When he eventually appeared on stage, Nero sang for hours, leaving the other contestants no time to perform. And with his supporters in the crowd making so much noise, Nero never bothered to wait for the judges' decision. He simply declared himself the winner.

Meanwhile all his mother could do was drink, and complain to anybody who would listen. She'd worked hard to win her son Rome's top job, and now he just abused the position. Soon, the Roman people began to call their Emperor 'Nero No-Talent' behind his back. They scrawled insensitive graffiti all over town: like 'Nero Sucks!' and 'Stop the Music!' Nero was deeply hurt. He blamed it all on his mum. She was really asking for it now. First he thought about bringing a lawsuit against her, or maybe even banishing her from Rome. But in the end, he decided just to kill her.

First he tried poison. He'd tested it on a pig, which died within minutes. Nero invited Agrippina over to dinner, and put some in her favourite cup. But it didn't work. He couldn't understand it. Next, he tried to fake an accident. Nero hired some carpenters, asking them to weaken the roof over his mother's bed so that the heavy wooden beams would fall on her during the night and splatter her across the rug. That didn't work either. The roof fell in during the day while his mother was in the garden. His next bright idea was a tragedy at sea. Nero had a special kind of ship made: one with an extremely weak and leaky hull. He gave the ship to his mother as an early birthday present. She was thrilled and quickly set sail on

MMM, THIS WINE IS DELIGHTFUL! NERO, YOU'VE FINALLY DONE SOMETHING RIGHT FOR A CHANGE.

a pleasure cruise. Just as Nero had planned, the ship sank on its maiden voyage. But then a dock servant rushed to Nero's palace, telling him that although the ship had sunk, his mother had saved herself by swimming to shore. The servant thought that this was good news; but Nero didn't agree. He was so furious he stabbed the poor man to death.

Still drenched in blood, Nero had another idea. He called his guards. Nero told them his mother had actually sent the messenger to assassinate him. The next day, Nero had his mum arrested on a charge of attempted murder. He threw her in the dungeon. About a week later, he paid the jailer to strangle her.

Now he could pursue his music career in peace.

Of course he told everyone she had committed suicide. The trouble was that no one believed him. All around town Romans scrawled graffiti: 'Nero murders!', 'Nero lies!' The young Emperor boiled with anger. Even from beyond the grave, his mother was still hurting his music career! He decided *everyone* in Rome was asking for it now. It was time to teach them all a lesson.

Nero sent his bouncers into the streets of Rome with blazing torches. Privately, he had always thought Rome had too many old buildings and too many narrow, winding streets. The city needed a makeover. He instructed his men to burn the whole place to the ground. A blazing inferno scorched Rome for six days and seven nights. Thousands of innocent people were killed, but Nero didn't care. They'd all been asking for it anyway, every last one of them! Nero watched the whole thing from his palace. While Rome burned and its people perished in the flames, Nero strummed his harp and recited poetry for his friends. Perhaps now, with everyone dead, he could pursue his music career in peace.

After the fire died down, the survivors were naturally quite peeved. They all knew that Nero was responsible. The Senate decided Nero was really asking for it. 'Some people are just better off dead,' they all agreed. They put out a contract out on the young Emperor. Nero was so terrified he went into hiding. Then, convinced that the people would find him sooner or later, he took up two daggers and forced them into his chest. He collapsed on the floor in a pool of his own blood. With the darkness closing around him, Nero moaned aloud: 'What a talent dies in me!'

JOSHUA WRIGHT was born in Geelong. He spent most of his time outside school playing in the paddocks out the back, building forts, crushing all sorts of random objects on the train line nearby and gathering cool stuff for cubby houses – car hulks, cow bones, sheep skulls, discarded *Playboys*, carpet samples, that kind of thing. His greatest passions were trains, cartoons, dinosaurs and *Star Wars*.

By high school, he was sure he wanted to be either a successful cartoonist or a big-budget Hollywood director. Later he took to writing crazy stories filled with mayhem and adventure. Two of these, *Plotless Pointless Pathetic* and *Hapless Hopeless Horrible*, have been published.

JOHN WRIGHT is Joshua's older brother. He says it was his idea to play forts, and he was the first to think of being a Hollywood director. He later changed his mind, and became an ancient history buff. He works at Birmingham University in England.

TIMELINE

BC

113   Barbarians defeat Romans in the Balkans

112   Rome begins war against King Jugurtha in North Africa

107   Gaius Marius is sent to Africa to fight Jugurtha

105   Gaius Marius and Lucius Sulla capture King Jugurtha

102–1   Gaius Marius returns and defeats two barbarian armies

100   Julius Caesar is born in Rome

89   King Mithradates of Pontus invades Roman lands in Asia

88   Lucius Sulla becomes General, is sent to fight Mithradates

87   Sulla goes to Greece and besieges Athens

87   Marius takes control of Rome

82   Sulla returns to Rome and takes over

81   Julius Caesar flees Rome

79   Lucius Sulla dies

78   Julius Caesar returns to Rome

73   Spartacus leads slave uprising

71   Crassus defeats slave army

62   Clodius violates the Bona Dea festival

61   Clodius bribes the jury and is acquitted in court

58   Julius Caesar leaves for France

58   Clodius chases Cicero out of Rome

53   Parthians defeat and kill Crassus

52   Clodius killed in street fighting outside Rome

49   Julius Caesar returns to Rome and takes over

44   Disgruntled Senators assassinate Julius Caesar

40   Antony and Augustus divide the Empire between them

31   Augustus defeats Antony & Cleopatra in sea battle at Actium

30   Augustus marches on Egypt, Antony & Cleopatra commit suicide

27   Augustus becomes Emperor

AD

14   Augustus dies, and his adopted son Tiberius becomes Emperor

37   Tiberius dies and his grand-nephew Caligula becomes Emperor

41   Caligula is murdered and his uncle Claudius becomes Emperor

54   Claudius is murdered and his stepson Nero becomes Emperor

64   Great Fire of Rome

68   Nero commits suicide

WHERE TO FIND OUT MORE

Websites

- http://www.bbc.co.uk/schools/romans/

  Contains information, pictures, games and activities on Roman civilisation

- http://www.historyforkids.org/learn/romans/index.htm

- http://www.roman-empire.net/

  Comprehensive information including maps, articles, timelines and images

- http://www.brims.co.uk/romans/

  Interactive site about Romans (especially the Romans in Britain); includes material prepared by schoolchildren, fascinating and disgusting facts, a quiz, and more information for parents and teachers

- http://www.jacksonesd.k12.or.us/k12projects/jimperry/rome.html

  Information on all aspects of Roman culture, including many pictures, via links to other sites.

- http://www.iol.ie/~coolmine/typ/romans/intro.html

  Explores aspects of the Roman way of life, such as clothes, entertainment, baths and theatres; no pictures

Books

Phillip Steele, *Find Out About: The Roman Empire*, Southwater, Sydney, 2000

Andrew Langley, *The Roman News*, Walker Books, London, 1998

Dyan Blacklock, *The Roman Army: the Legendary Soldiers Who Created an Empire*, Omnibus Books, Adelaide, 2004

For teachers

Primary sources, all published as Penguin Classics

Plutarch, *Makers of Rome*

Plutarch, *Fall of the Roman Republic*

Suetonius, *The Twelve Caesars*

Tacitus, *The Annals of Imperial Rome*

Modern books

Jo-Ann Shelton, *As the Romans Did: A Source Book in Roman Social History*, 2nd edn, Oxford University Press, Oxford and New York, 1997

Allen M. Ward, Fritz M. Heichelheim, Cedric A. Yeo, *A History of the Roman People*, 4th edn, Prentice-Hall, Upper Saddle River, 2002

INDEX